BETTER BUSINESS WRITING

Techniques for Improving Correspondence

THIRD EDITION

Susan Brock

A FIFTY-MINUTE™ SERIES BOOK

BETTER BUSINESS WRITING
Techniques for Improving Correspondence
THIRD EDITION

Susan Brock

CREDITS:
Editor: **Michael G. Crisp**
Designer: **Carol Harris**
Typesetting: **ExecuStaff**
Cover Design: **Fifth Street Design**
Artwork: **Ralph Mapson**

© 1996 by Crisp Publications, Inc.
Printed in the United States of America by Von Hoffmann Graphics, Inc.

CrispLearning.com

00 01 02 03   10 9 8 7 6 5 4

Library of Congress Catalog Card Number 96-85351
Brock, Susan
Better Business Writing—Third Edition
ISBN 1-56052-396-4

This book is printed on recyclable paper with soy ink.

LEARNING OBJECTIVES FOR:

BETTER BUSINESS WRITING
THIRD EDITION

The objectives for *Better Business Writing—Third Edition* are listed below. They have been developed to guide you, the reader, to the core issues covered in this book.

Objectives

❑ 1) **To explain how understanding personality types can improve your business communication**

❑ 2) **To review the basics of spelling, punctuation, and usage**

❑ 3) **To explain style in writing**

❑ 4) **To discuss persuasive writing**

Assessing Your Progress

In addition to the learning objectives, Crisp Learning has developed an **assessment** that covers the fundamental information presented in this book. A twenty-five item, multiple choice/true-false question-naire allows the reader to evaluate his or her comprehension of the subject matter. An answer sheet with a chart matching the questions to the listed objectives is also available. To learn how to obtain a copy of this assessment, please call **1-800-442-7477** and ask to speak with a Customer Service Representative.

Assessments should not be used in any selection process.

ABOUT THE AUTHOR

Susan Brock has led Coopers & Lybrand's San Francisco-based communication practice for the past eight years. Along with helping organizations communicate more effectively with their employees, Sue has taught business writing at the college level for the past 10 years. She is also the author of *Writing Business Proposals and Reports* and the co-author of *Writing A Human Resource Manual,* two other Crisp books.

CONTENTS

CONTENTS (continued)

PREFACE

American businesses reportedly lose $1 billion a year due to "foggy" writing that wastes time, kills contracts, and alienates customers. You don't have to be part of this problem. This book is designed to teach you the basics you need to become a better writer. The accompanying exercises will enhance your writing skills and are relevant to the practical demands of the business world. By the time you complete this brief book, you will be better prepared to write a clear, concise business letter, memo, and report.

The best way to improve your writing is to write often. You'll find if you routinely practice the techniques in this book, your writing skills will continue to improve. When this happens, you're on your way to writing more clearly, concisely, and humanely, and this will make you more effective at work.

A voluntary learning contract is available on page 79. It is a good starting point if you are serious about getting the most from this book. Good luck and don't give up! Writing well is hard work, but your career is worth it.

Susan Brock

HOW WELL DO YOU KNOW YOUR WRITING ABILITIES?

Before you begin, take a minute to assess your writing style. You may discover that you know a lot more than you think, or you may discover specific areas where you need to improve. Either way, this exercise will help you assess your writing ability. Read each statement, and mark the response that applies to you.

	YES	NO	I DON'T KNOW
1. I write from my reader's perspective.	☐	☐	☐
2. I have no problem with the basics: grammar, spelling, and punctuation.	☐	☐	☐
3. I know the difference between active and passive construction.	☐	☐	☐
4. I try to choose simple words to communicate clearly.	☐	☐	☐
5. I make it a point to state clearly the specific purpose of my letters or memos.	☐	☐	☐
6. I recognize and avoid business clichés and jargon.	☐	☐	☐
7. I ruthlessly edit everything I write.	☐	☐	☐
8. I'm confident I can communicate persuasively.	☐	☐	☐

Don't worry if you weren't sure of the significance of any of the above questions. As you proceed through this book you will read explanations of each. Soon you'll be able to mark each statement in this self-assessment with a YES!

P A R T

I

Back to the Basics

THE BASICS—SPELLING, PUNCTUATION, AND USAGE

You may be approaching this section with discomfort. Despite your fears, you will find it is relatively painless—in part because it's short, and because it concentrates only on the most common errors people make. The basics include spelling, punctuation, and usage. We'll briefly review each.

Many people acquire bad habits in mechanics and usage before leaving school. The purpose of this section is to strengthen your skills in the basics. If this section does nothing more than correct a single error you repeatedly make, your writing will improve because of it.

THREE TIPS FOR BETTER SPELLING

If spelling is not your strong suit, you might find the following information helpful.

How many times have you checked a word in a dictionary, only to refer to a dictionary again for the same word because you couldn't remember the correct spelling? Following are three tips to help you correctly spell some problem words.

SPELLING BASICS

Sometimes all we need to correct an error we make regularly is to use a mnemonic (memory aid) device.

1. Basic Method to Help Your Memory

- Use a dictionary
- Look at the word in syllables
- Say it aloud in syllables
- Visualize and say aloud
- Write it out fully

This method involves the use of five senses to aid your memory (seeing, saying, hearing, visualizing, writing).

2. Shortcuts Method for Your Most Troublesome Words

- Locate the trouble spot in a word (the place where you misspell it)
- Isolate the sound
- Underline the trouble spot
- Emphasize it by mispronouncing it with the correct letter sound

    SEP–A–RATE; FA–TI–GUE

- Look for short words in the long word

    ARGUMENT (GUM)

    ENVIRONMENT (IRON)

    CEMETERY (MET)

3. Gimmicks

You can also make up your own gimmick to help you remember how to spell words that are troublesome for you. Here are a few ideas:

- Question: What would you yell in a cemetery? Answer: Eee! (Remember that "cemetery" has three e's.)

- The accident occurred on the RR tracks. (Remember that "occurred" has two r's.)

- Loose as a goose. (Use rhymes to remember that "loose" has two o's.)

- A Rat In The House Might Eat The Ice Cream (Use acronyms: the first letter of each word spells "arithmetic".)

- The capitol building has a dome. (Remember that "capitol" when referring to the building is spelled with an "ol" instead of an "al".)

SPELLING TRICKS

1. Remember This Rhyme from Grammar School?

Use "i" before "e"

Except after "c"

And when sounded like "a"

As in "neighbor" and "weigh"

This spelling rule applies to more than 1,000 words. Can you think of some exceptions to the rule? Here are a few: *neither, weird, sheik, either, seize, leisure.*

THREE TIPS FOR BETTER SPELLING (continued)

2. To Double Or Not to Double?

Occurred or occured? Which is it? Do you have trouble remembering if words like "occur" have one or two r's before adding an ending, such as "ed"? Here's a trick. Take a look at the following lists of words:

Accent on First Syllable	Accent on Second Syllable
layering	occurred
offered	referring
traveled	preferred
canceled	remitting
benefited	omitted
totaled	permitted

Notice that the words on the first list do not double the last consonant before adding "ing" or "ed," and the words on the second list do double the last consonant. One reason "offered" does not double the "r" and "referred" does is because you pronounce "offer" with the accent (or stress) on the first syllable. Say it out loud (OFF' er). Now say "refer" out loud (re FER').

- If the accent is on the first syllable, do not double the final consonant.

- If the accent is on the second syllable, DO double the final consonant.

SPECIAL NOTE: Some words may be spelled either way. For example:

canceled or cancelled

traveled or travelled

programed or programmed

If you're in doubt, check your dictionary. But if you use the doubling rule, you don't have to remember which words can be spelled either way. By following the rule, you'll be able to figure out when to double and when not to. This doubling rule applies to more than 3,000 words.

3. Endings: Is It •*able* or •*ible*?

You add *-able* to a full word.

adapt = adaptable

work = workable

love = lovable [NOTE: drop the e before adding the ending]

desire = desirable [Again, drop the second e before the ending]

You add *-ible* if the root word is not a word by itself.

credible ["cred" is not a word when it stands by itself]

tangible

You add *-ible* to words that end in x, ns and miss.

flexible

responsible

permissible

For the Computer Savvy: About Spellchecks

Many computer software programs have a spellcheck feature, which will highlight words that are not in the computer's dictionary. Highlighted words could include misspelled words, proper names such as ACME Corporation, and initials or acronyms such as HMO, CPA and NASA. The good news is that spellcheck will find and correct many words you've misspelled. It will not, however, find and correct those words you've *misused* but not misspelled, such as the following.

affect	instead of	effect
there	instead of	their or they're
to	instead of	too or two
where	instead of	wear
imply	instead of	infer
bear	instead of	bare
wry	instead of	rye
compliment	instead of	complement
comprise	instead of	compose
manger	instead of	manager

In short, a spellcheck can be a useful tool, but it's no substitute for careful proofreading!

EXERCISE: *Spelling*

DIRECTIONS: *Fill in the missing letters to spell the word correctly. Check your answers with those on page 83.*

1. Many companies want to hire people who are _____ (flex-ble).

2. Ms. Brown wanted us to sit _____ (tog-th-r) at the meeting so we would not be _____ (sep-r-ted) when the meeting was over.

3. The new hotel can _____ (acco-date) up to 1,500 guests.

4. This memo _____ (super-edes) the _____ (prec-ding) one, which was distributed last week.

5. The hospital _____ (ben-fit) raised a lot of money for the children's wing.

6. It never _____ (oc-ur-ed) to us that the _____ (gove-ment) might increase our taxes.

7. The secretary's boss _____ (of-er-ed) her a bonus if she would _____ (proc-d) to enroll in a shorthand class.

8. We avoided an _____ (arg-ment) when we discussed changing the _____ (envi-ment) of the office to boost employee morale.

9. The hinges on the door are _____ (l-se), and it _____ (consist-ntly) rattles when opened.

10. It would be difficult not to _____ (bel-ve) the results.

PUNCTUATION POINTERS

With spelling, people usually fall into one of two categories—good spellers or poor spellers. Punctuation errors, on the other hand, can trouble everyone.

> **COMMA (,)**
> **SEMICOLON (;)**
> **COLON (:)**
> **APOSTROPHE (')**

Fortunately, of the 30 main punctuation marks, business writing requires fewer than a dozen. Of these, the comma, colon, semicolon, and apostrophe are used most often—and often incorrectly!

These are the four punctuation marks we have chosen to cover. As you read the next few pages, you'll see that we have touched on only the highlights of punctuation pointers, but we hope we've included solutions to some of the problems that trouble you.

PUNCTUATION POINTERS (continued)

COMMA (,)

The comma sets off or separates words or groups of words within sentences.

Six Rules for the Comma

➤ Use a comma after a long introductory phrase.

> *After working all day at the office, I went home for dinner.*

➤ If the introductory phrase is short, forget the comma.

> *After work I went home for dinner.*

➤ Use the comma if the sentence would be confusing without it.

> *The day before, I borrowed her calculator.*
>
> *When you've finished, your dinner is ready.*

➤ Use a comma to separate items in a series.

> *I need to pack my computer, calculator, business cards, and toothbrush.*

➤ Use a comma to separate two sentences that are joined by a*nd, but, or, nor, for, so, yet.*

> *He wanted the promotion, but he was afraid to ask his boss.*
>
> *She like her new job, and she respected her colleagues.*
>
> *They may go to the game, or they may stay here.*
>
> *The partners aren't going to the retreat, nor are they happy about it.*
>
> *Her assistant took a cab, for it was a long way to walk.*
>
> *They waited until Friday, so it was too late to go.*
>
> *I'd like to travel, yet I'm reluctant to change jobs.*

➤ Use a comma to set off nonessential elements in a sentence.

> *At the podium stood a man wearing a green tie.*
>
> *At the podium stood Frank, wearing a green tie.*

In the first sentence, "wearing a green tie" is used to identify a specific man. Without it, the reader wouldn't know whom the writer was referring to, so it's essential to the meaning of the sentence.

In the second sentence, the writer assumes the reader knows Frank. "Wearing a green tie" adds only descriptive information about Frank, but it's not essential to the meaning of the sentence.

Here's another example.

The computer that's in the hallway is brand new. (The writer identifies one particular computer "in the hallway," rather than the computer that's somewhere else. The location is essential to the sentence.)

The computer, which is in the hallway, is brand new. (The writer assumes there's only one computer and adds only descriptive information—"in the hallway"—that's nonessential to the meaning of the sentence.)

A Comma No-No

Do not separate two independent statements with a comma.

He bought his first car last fall, it never ran well.

You can correct this sentence in any of the following ways.

1. Use a period in place of the comma

   He bought his first car last fall. It never ran well.

2. Use a comma plus a conjunction (and, but, or, nor, so, for, yet)

   He bought his first car last fall, but it never ran well.

3. Use a semicolon

   He bought his first car last fall; it never ran well.

PUNCTUATION POINTERS (continued)

SEMICOLON (;)

The semicolon separates two independent clauses, but it keeps those two thoughts more tightly linked than a period can: "I type letters; he types bills." Use a semicolon *before* and a comma *after* the following words if the words come between two independent clauses.

accordingly	hence	moreover	similarly
also	however	namely	still
besides	likewise	nevertheless	then
consequently	indeed	nonetheless	therefore
furthermore	instead	otherwise	thus

I thought I had completed the project; consequently, I was surprised to hear about the additional work.

We have prepared your estimate; however, you should sign it by Friday.

The partners' retreat will be held in March; therefore, all business matters will be discussed then.

COLON (:)

A colon is a tip-off to get ready for what's next: a list, a long quotation, or an explanation. A colon separates independent clauses when the second clause explains or amplifies the first.

Fred was proud of his sister: she had been promoted to managing partner.

My new office contains the following items: a partner's desk, a leather chair, and oak paneling.

There are two things to remember in a job interview: always arrive promptly and always dress appropriately.

APOSTROPHE (')

An apostrophe is used to form the possessive of nouns and some pronouns and to mark the omission of letter(s) in a contraction.

► If the noun is singular, add 's.

I enjoyed Betty's presentation.

Someone's coat is in the lobby.

► The same applies for singular nouns ending in "s" like James.

This is James's new office.

► If the noun is plural, add an apostrophe after the s:

Those are the clients' files.

► If the singular noun ends in "s" (like "Jones"), add "es" and an apostrophe to make it both plural and possessive.

Here is the Joneses' tax information.

EXERCISE: *Punctuation*

DIRECTIONS: *Punctuate the following; then compare your answers with those on page 84. Not all of the sentences need additional punctuation.*

1. The executive watched the competition but the competition went ahead with the takeover.

2. During our meeting she was genial but shrewd.

3. Today more women are becoming executives in corporations.

4. The job was difficult therefore he quit.

5. My suitcase contained files pencils books and paper.

6. We thought we would have to work late consequently we were happy to be home before dark.

7. My boss car was in the shop however she borrowed her husbands.

8. In preparation for the meeting Mr. Jones asked us to do three things set up the equipment dust the tables and empty the ashtrays.

9. We wanted to go to the partners meeting but we were unable to leave before the weekend.

10. Lois résumé arrived yesterday moreover she phoned for an interview next week.

EXERCISE: *Spelling and Punctuation*

DIRECTIONS. *Correct any incorrect punctuation and spelling in the following letter; then compare your answers with those on page 85.*

Southwestern Corporation 333 LaSalle Street, Chicago Illinois

March 29, 19XX

Mr. John C. Fremont
2929 East Sycamore Street
Chicago IL 60601

Dear Mr. Freemont:

Thank you for meeting with us, and for your time and effort in preparing for the intervue. We appreciate your accomodating us with a flexable schedule.

We are in the final stages of procesing your application and we need three more items for our files. Your social security number permanent home address and your date of birth; as soon as we get this information we can procede to complete your permanent records.

Everyone here at Southwestern Corporation is looking forward to working with you. And we are eager to have you begin as soon as possible. Please, call me as soon as you can with this information.

Sincerely,

Janet L. Estes
Senor Vice President

/jle

PROPER WORD USAGE

People sometimes have trouble choosing the most accurate or appropriate word—especially when many words sound alike. Fortunately, several books contain a lot of information on proper word usage. For example, *The Elements of Style 3rd Edition* by William Strunk and E. B. White (MacMillan Publishing Co., Inc., New York) and *On Writing Well* (Third Edition) by William Zinsser (Harper & Row, Publishers, New York). Both are interesting, easy to read, and packed with information.

A Usage Quiz

INSTRUCTIONS: *Read each item below and circle or fill in the correct answer(s). After you complete the quiz, turn to page 86 and compare your answers with those of the author's.*

1. Which is correct?

The (**effect** or **affect**) of wearing seatbelts can (**effect** or **affect**) the number of people injured in automobile accidents.

2. Which is correct?

Lee Iacocca singlehandedly (**effected** or **affected**) the turnaround of Chrysler Corporation, which had a dramatic (**effect** or **affect**) on the production of U.S.-made automobiles.

3. Which is correct?

  a. The party pledges not to raise taxes, which would be harmful to the economy.

  b. The party pledges not to raise taxes that would be harmful to the economy.

4. Which is correct?

  a. An historic choice.

  b. A historic choice.

5. Which is correct?

  a. He implied that we were not to blame.

  b. He inferred that we were not to blame.

6. Which is correct?

This memo will (**supercede** or **supersede**) the one we wrote last week.

7. Which is correct?

There (**seem** or **seems**) to be problems with the way management has handled billings.

8. Which is correct?

Neither my boss nor the partners (**goes** or **go**) to the meetings.

9. Which is correct?

The (**affect** or **effect**) of lower interest rates will (**affect** or **effect**) our money market investments.

10. Complete each sentence using either *capital* or *capitol*.

Austin is the _____ of Texas.

The company tried to raise enough _____ to buy new equipment.

Paris is the _____ of France.

The first word of every sentence should begin with a _____ letter.

The senator met with the press on the steps of the _____ building.

P A R T

II

Your Writing Style:
Choose Words
Carefully

YOUR WRITING STYLE

The word "style" means how language is used. Although a sentence or phrase can be stated in endless ways and most people will understand what you mean, avoiding the most common pitfalls of writing will give your work clarity, crispness, and greater force. Twelve frequently made errors and how to avoid them are discussed on the next pages.

PITFALLS OF BUSINESS WRITING

Following is a list of 12 common problems in business writing, followed by more detailed descriptions of each pitfall. You are invited to make this list more personal by jotting down other examples you've encountered.

PITFALLS OF BUSINESS WRITING

1. Too Many Words

2. Clichés

3. Too Many Big Words

4. Jargon

5. Vague Expressions

6. Condescending Statements

7. Sexist Language

8. Negative Expressions

9. Inattention to Detail

10. Inattention to the Reader

11. Lack of Commitment

12. Passive Construction

_____

_____

1. Too Many Words

- One word is better than two

- A good rule is to limit your sentences to fewer than 17 words

- Edit ruthlessly

> *NOT:* In this letter we have attempted to answer all of your questions, and we hope that if you have any additional questions whatsoever, you will not hesitate to contact us.
>
> *BUT:* If you have additional questions, please call us.

2. Clichés

- Avoid fad words and trite phrases like "input," "parameters," "utilize," "hopefully," and "enclosed please find"

> *NOT:* Enclosed please find the information per your request. Hopefully, you can utilize our product to benefit your company within the parameters of your computer's invoice processing. We appreciate your input.
>
> *BUT:* We have enclosed the information you requested. Our product will speed your computer's invoice processing. Thank you for your suggestions.

3. Too Many Big Words

- Keep your writing simple: use "home" instead of "abode," "face" instead of "visage," "use" instead of "utilize"

- Short words are better than long words

- Try to be natural in your writing

- Read your letters aloud after you write them; they should sound human and conversational

> *NOT:* Pursuant to our discussion, herewith we acknowledge receipt of your correspondence as of the above date.
>
> *BUT:* We received your letter on December 16 as we discussed.

PITFALLS OF BUSINESS WRITING
(continued)

4. Jargon

- Avoid unexplained terms like "facilitator" and "interface"

What is a "modified departmentalized schedule"?

> *NOT:* Our facilitator will interface with the new communication systems network.
>
> *BUT:* Our administrative assistant will operate the new telephone system.

5. Vague Expressions

- Be concise and specific

If the "profits were affected" did they increase or decrease?

> *NOT:* The company's negative cash flow position forced it to resize its operations to the level of profitable market opportunities.
>
> *BUT:* The company lost money and had to lay off workers.

6. Condescending Statements

- Write with warmth, as one human to another

"Of course" can be interpreted "as any idiot knows."

> *NOT:* We are certain you are concerned with saving money. Of course, you will mail the enclosed card. We thank you in advance.
>
> *BUT:* If saving money is important to you, please mail the enclosed card today. Thank you.

7. Sexist Language (see page 36 for more information on this)

- Consider your reader (the salutation "Gentlemen" is outdated)

- Traditionally, "he," "his," and "him" were neutral pronouns, yet there are alternatives you can use to avoid offending your reader

- Use "he or she" sparingly

> *NOT:* An accountant must pass a difficult exam before he can become a CPA.
>
> *BUT:* (*use plurals*) Accountants must pass a difficult exam before they can become CPAs.
>
> *OR* (*avoid using pronouns whenever possible*) An accountant must pass a difficult exam before becoming a CPA.
>
> *OR* To become a CPA, an accountant must pass a difficult exam.
>
> *OR* (*use "you" when appropriate—if you know your audience!*) As an accountant, you must pass a difficult exam before you become a CPA.

8. Negative Expressions

- Stress the positive

- Instead of telling what you can't do or don't have, provide good news

> *NOT:* We're sorry to tell you that we don't carry XYZ software.
>
> *BUT:* Since we no longer carry XYZ software, we are sending you a list of distributors who do carry the software.

PITFALLS OF BUSINESS WRITING
(continued)

9. Inattention to Detail

- Triple check accuracy and quality
- Reread for typos and misspelled words

> *NOT:* We hope we can accomodate your office supply and stationary needs.
>
> *BUT:* We hope we can accommodate your office supply and stationery needs.

10. Inattention to the Reader

- Write in the first person when appropriate
- Write in the second person when possible
- Remember to write from the reader's perspective

> *NOT:* We would like to invite you to attend the conference.
>
> *BUT:* You are invited to attend the conference.

11. Lack of Commitment

- Take a stand
- Omit qualifiers—"sort of," "rather," "quite," "somewhat"

> *NOT:* We are quite pleased about our rather exciting word processor.
>
> *BUT:* We are pleased about our exciting line of word processors.

12. Passive Construction

- Use active verbs

- The normal order of sentences is subject (performer of action), verb, and object (receiver of action). In passive construction, the order is *reversed:* the object is first, followed by a form of the verb "be" (am, is, are, was, were, been, being) before the main verb. The subject is last (usually preceded by the word "by").

PASSIVE: The check was signed by my boss. [7 words]

The letter is being typed by the secretary. [8 words]

He practices what has been learned. ["By him" is implied.]

ACTIVE: My boss signed the check. [5 words]

The secretary is typing the letter. [6 words]

He practices what he has learned.

- Sometimes writers use passive construction and leave out the subject of the sentence

---

PASSIVE: An employee's extra efforts should be recognized. [By whom?]

ACTIVE: Bosses should recognize an employee's extra efforts.

PASSIVE: Enclosed are your schedules.

ACTIVE: I enclose your schedules.

- Active construction is almost always more direct, more economical, and more forceful than passive construction

- As you proofread your work, consider making your writing more active by the following:

    1. State the subject of each sentence

    2. Place the subject of each sentence before the object

    3. Use the verb "be" cautiously—overuse weakens your writing

EXERCISE: Wordiness 1

How can you simplify to improve the expressions on this list? This exercise will help you identify and eliminate wordiness.

terminate the illumination	lights out
revenue commitment	tax increase
at this point in time	
in the event of	
due to the fact that	
at a later date	
jumped off of	
on a daily basis	
each and every one	
firstly	
in my opinion, I think	
irregardless	
owing to the fact that	
there is no doubt but that	
so very happy	
clenched tightly	
close proximity	
close scrutiny	
in the majority of instances	
at this juncture of maturation	
in an intelligent manner	

Compare your answers with those of the author on page 88.

(UNNECESSARY) REDUNDANCIES

Sometimes people use too many words because of redundant expressions. Look closely at the list below. Many of these expressions sound right because we hear them so often, but notice how many words we can eliminate with no loss in meaning.

The following list contains common redundant expressions. Delete the word or words in parentheses.

(advance) planning	(as) for example
ask (a question)	refer (back)
(as to) whether	(true) facts
(as) yet	(when and) if
(at a) later (date)	whether (or not)
at (the) present (time)	written (down)
(basic) fundamentals	(brief) moment
(specific) example	off (of)
(but) nevertheless	period (of time)
(close) proximity	might (possibly)
(close) scrutiny	since (the time when)
combine (together)	recur (again)
(completely) filled	(still) remains
consensus (of opinion)	(thorough) investigation
continue (on)	sufficient (enough)
estimated at (about)	started (off) with
(exact) opposites	merged (together)
first (of all)	repeat (again)
for (a period of) 10 days	blend (together)
(just) exactly	came (at a time) when
my (personal) opinion	(false) pretenses
(absolutely) essential	(on a) daily (basis)

EXERCISE: Wordiness 2

Now that you've learned to recognize and eliminate wordiness, this exercise provides additional practice pruning what your write. You may rewrite each, but make sure that the original meaning is not lost. After you've completed the exercise, turn to page 89 and compare your answers with those of the author.

1. It has been my wish for a considerable period of time to gain entrance into the field of accounting. This is due to the fact that challenges of my intellect are what challenge me.

2. To me it appears that Smith did not give attention whatsoever to the suggestion that had been recommended by the consultant.

3. In the past there were a quite large number of firms located on the West Coast offering us competition. At this present point in time, the majority of those firms have been forced to go out of business by the hardships and difficulties of the present recessionary period of business contraction and stagnation.

4. It is the policy of this company in every case to proceed with care in testing each and every new product under development by us, and such testing must precede our arriving at any positive conclusion with respect to the effectiveness of said product.

5. In the event that Wilkins does not come forth with an expression of willingness to lend us assistance in the matter of financing this project, it is entirely conceivable that we will not be able to make the required acquisitions of raw materials we need without help.

Passive Voice—An Active Writing Exercise

Revise the following sentences so that all main verbs are in the active voice. Leave the space blank if the sentence is already in the active voice. See the author's solutions on page 90.

EXAMPLE:

The consultant was hired by the manager.

The manager hired the consultant.

1. Our request for an increase in salary will be considered by the board at its next meeting.

2. Our inability to agree is seen by management as a weakness.

3. The decision on the annual budget is always made by our board of directors.

4. Incorrect data on the computer should be deleted.

5. Our office manager will speak to us on Monday.

6. It will be necessary to downsize the company's marketing department.

7. Problems should be reported to the office manager.

8. The check was signed by my boss.

9. Please be advised that these adjustments should be completed immediately.

10. The jobs were completed by the management team.

PARALLEL CONSTRUCTION

Parallel construction adds clarity, elegance, and symmetry to your writing. Words, phrases, and statements are coordinated to be grammatically parallel: noun aligned with noun, verb with verb, and phrase with phrase. For example:

1. *NOT:* Speaking in public is sometimes harder than to write in private.

    BUT: Speaking in public is sometimes harder than writing in private.

2. *NOT:* My partner is a man of action, decision, and who is bright.

    BUT: My partner is a man of action, decision, and intelligence.

3. *NOT:* Sarah's office was painted, had carpeting put in and paneled last week.

    BUT: Sarah's office was painted, carpeted, and paneled last week.

4. *NOT:* To teach, to supervise, and delegating work are a few of the tasks our office manager performs.

    BUT: To teach, to supervise, and to delegate work are a few of the tasks our office manager performs.

    OR: Teaching, supervising, and delegating work are a few of the tasks our office manager performs.

Not only does parallel construction add symmetry, it often reduces wordiness—see examples #2 and #3 above. Don't hesitate, however, to repeat a word if it makes your sentence clearer. For example:

1. *NOT:* She has and continues to seem competent:

    BUT: She has seemed and continues to seem competent.

2. *NOT:* A secretary can program a computer to type a letter but not think.

    BUT: A secretary can program a computer to type a letter but not to think.

When you proofread your work, check for parallel construction. The added clarity and economy will add polish to your style.

EXERCISE: *Parallel Writing*

DIRECTIONS: *Revise the following sentences to form correct parallel construction. If the sentence is already parallel, leave the space blank.*

1. It was both a long meeting and very tedious.

2. Joe likes a job with challenging work that keeps him stimulated.

3. Poor writing wastes time, costs money, and customers feel alienated.

4. Speaking in public is sometimes harder than writing in private.

5. My partner is a man of action, decision, and who is bright.

6. This would eliminate continual errors, repeated corrections, unnecessary memos, and, most important, the time spent on each.

7. His experience made him sullen, bitter, and a cynic.

8. Our instructor drilled us, tested us, and he also gave us encouragement.

EXERCISE (continued)

9. I went to Maui to enjoy the warm weather and for getting some practice in snorkeling.

10. I plunged into the water, swam away from shore, and made my first dive.

11. Our first choice is John, who is healthy, witty, capable, and an athlete.

12. The personnel officer told me that the clerk would answer the phone, greet the visitors, distribute mail, and some typing.

13. On a resume:

> Hobbies: swimming, reading, cycling, and piano

14. On an overhead transparency during a business presentation:

> WHAT WE CAN DO FOR YOU:
> Increase your cashflow
> Improve your customer relationships
> Reduce employee turnover
> More new business

15. Sometimes going to meetings is as exciting as watching paint dry.

RECOGNIZING CLICHÉS

Learn to recognize and avoid trite expressions and clichés. Examples include:

- along these lines
- as per our agreement
- at the present time
- due to the fact that
- enclosed please find
- for the purpose of
- in response to your memo of
- in view of the fact
- per
- pursuant to
- regarding the matter of
- we are returning some herewith

- as per your request
- at an early date
- despite the fact that
- enclosed herewith
- for the amount of
- in response to your letter of
- pending receipt of
- please be advised
- thank you for your cooperation
- we will file your letter for future reference
- with reference to your letter of
- subsequent to

AVOIDING SEXISM

The increasing number of women in business has changed many traditional practices. One change is the updating of business correspondence to include women. For decades the salutation in most letters was "Gentlemen." Because this is no longer suitable, use a more specific—and nonsexist—form of address in the salutation.

INSTEAD OF:	USE:
Gentlemen:	Dear Partners:
	Dear Doctors:
	Dear Directors:
	Dear Educators:
	Dear Shareholders:
	Dear Members:
	add your own _____

Many companies omit the salutation and complimentary close. Letters are simplified to emphasize their message and streamline their form. The following letter demonstrates this idea.

March 26, 19XX

Personnel Manager
Sanders Enterprises, Inc.
1425 Seaview Way
Daily City, CA 93456

SPECIAL PHONE SYSTEM*

We have established a special phone system to improve the communication between employment counselors and employers. Please call our office any afternoon between 4:00–5:00 if you have questions about available applicants or if you would just like to talk. We believe that if we encourage employers to call, we can establish a closer relationship with you and better meet your staffing needs.

Ted F. Jones
Employment Counselor

---

*This subject line may be placed flush left to conform with the block style of the letter or be centered as it is here.

PART

III

Improving Your Business Writing

BUSINESS WRITING

This section contains writing samples of letters and memos that exemplify weaknesses and errors common in business writing. Some of the weaknesses are more subtle than others. Please read each sample carefully, and evaluate each stage: the "before" version, the "corrected" version, and the "improved" version.

Writing Samples

DESCRIPTION: *John Freeman, president of ABC Enterprises, requested his accountant to explain why his accounting bill doubled since last year. Following is the accountant's response.*

BEFORE

XYZ ACCOUNTING CORPORATION
1420 Fremont Way
Oakdale, CA 95123
(805) 555-4322

July 2, 19XX

Mr. John Freeman
ABC Enterprises

Dear John:

In response to your letter of June 15, 19XX, enclosed please find Exhibit A. As you can see, the work performed for you this year is different than last year. In addition, the parameters of tasks increased since last year. Accordingly due to this fact and the fact that our billing rates were raised this year; it was necessary to increase our charges for professional services rendered. Hopefully, this letter offers some explanation as to the question you raised. If you require more additional information, please don't hesitate to contact us.

Sincerely,

XYZ Accounting Corporation

BUSINESS WRITING (continued)

CORRECTED

XYZ ACCOUNTING CORPORATION
1420 Fremont Way
Oakdale, CA 95123
(805) 555-4322

July 2, 19XX

Mr. John Freeman
ABC Enterprises
2027 Washington Blvd.
Oakdale, CA 95123

Dear John:

~trite~ ~condescending~ ~cliché~

In response to your letter of June 15, 19XX, enclosed please find Exhibit A. As you can see, the work performed for you this year is different than last year. *[use "from"]* In addition, the parameters *[JARGON]* of tasks increased since last year. *[omit]* Accordingly due to this fact and the fact that our billing rates were raised this year; it was necessary *[PASSIVE]* to increase our charges for professional services rendered. Hopefully, *[omit]* this letter offers some explanation as to the question you raised. If you require more additional *[redundant]* information, please don't hesitate to contact us. *[use "Answers"]*

wordy

Sincerely,

XYZ Accounting Corporation

IMPROVED

XYZ ACCOUNTING CORPORATION
1420 Fremont Way
Oakdale, CA 95123
(805) 555-4322

June 25, 19XX

Mr. John Freeman
ABC Enterprises
1000 Welch Way
Fountain Canyon, AZ 84666

Dear John:

We understand your concern, and we hope the following will answer your questions regarding the increase in your bill.

1. Last year we spent 12 hours (@ $200/hour) preparing two tax returns for you.

2. This year we spent 15 hours (@ $250/hour) preparing four tax returns for you.

3. This year we successfully represented you in an audit with the Internal Revenue Service (3 hours @ $250/hour).

4. This year we produced monthly financial statements for you, whereas last year we produced quarterly financial statements.

Please call me if you would like to discuss this further. We value you as a client.

Sincerely,

XYZ Accounting Corporation

by Marianne Evers, CPA

ME/jdc

BUSINESS WRITING (continued)

EMPLOYMENT AGENCY COUNSELOR'S LETTER: Following is a letter from an employment agency counselor to businesses announcing a new telephone communication setup.

BEFORE

September 5, 19XX

Dear Employer:

We have established a special phone communication system to provide additional opportunities for your input. During this year we will give added emphasis to the goal of communication and utilize a variety of means to accomplish this goal. Your input, from the unique position of employer, will help us to plan and implement an effective plan that meets the staffing needs of your company. An open dialogue, feedback and sharing of information between employment counselors and employers will enable us to work with your staffing needs in the most effective manner.

Sincerely,

Ted F. Jones
Employment Counselor

CORRECTED

September 5, 19XX

Dear Employer:

jargon — *use "use"* — *vague* — *jargon*

We have established a (special phone communication system) to provide additional opportunities for your (input.) During this year we will give added emphasis to the goal of communication and (utilize) a variety of means to accomplish this goal. Your (input) from the (unique position) of employer, will help us to plan and (implement) an effective plan that meets the staffing needs of your company. An open dialogue,(feedback and sharing of information) between employment counselors and employers will enable us to work with your staffing needs (in the most effective manner.)

wordy — *unclear* — *stilted*

Sincerely,

Ted F. Jones
Employment Counselor

IMPROVED

September 5, 19XX

Dear Employer:

We have established a special phone system to improve the communication between employment counselors and employers. Please call our office any afternoon between 4:00–5:00 if you have questions about available applicants or if you'd just like to talk. We believe that if we encourage you to call, we can establish a closer relationship and better meet your staffing needs.

Sincerely,

Ted F. Jones
Employment Counselor

This revised version of the letter sounds much more human.

BUSINESS WRITING (continued)

Memo

A sales manager asked his administrative assistant to send a memo (with a copy of quarterly sales figures) to the sales staff asking them to meet with him on the following Friday. The result follows.

BEFORE

MEMORANDUM

TO: All Sales Representatives

FROM: Jim Martin

DATE: July 15, 19XX

SUBJ: Sales Meeting

Re phone contact of July 8, final sales totals for the quarter ended June are enclosed herewith. A planning conference for all sales personnel will be scheduled for the near future and these figures will be discussed. It is hoped that all district managers will be aware that the figures are such that reductions in the total number of dealerships and retail units may be indicated. A meeting to discuss this matter will be held on Friday, 18 July, at 3 p.m., in the regional manager's office. Thank you for your cooperation.

IMPROVED

MEMORANDUM

    TO: All Sales Representatives

FROM: Jim Martin

DATE: July 15, 19XX

ᏟUᎠᎫ. Ꮞales Meeting

Please attend a sales meeting on Friday, July 18 at 3 p.m. in the regional manager's office. We will discuss the attached quarterly sales totals.

This meeting is important because we may have to reduce dealerships and retail units.

Note how direct and clear the revised version is. The sentences are brief and to the point, and the revised version is more natural and conversational without sounding too informal.

NINE TIPS FOR A BETTER MEMO

1. Get to the point quickly—the reader already knows the purpose of the memo because of the subject line.

2. Be interesting, conversational, and natural.

3. Highlight key ideas (*, –, or •); make it readable.

4. Keep it short—use 17 or fewer words per sentence generally.

5. Write in A–B–C order (sequentially).

6. Be specific, clear, concise, and economical.

7. Keep your reader(s) in mind.

8. Keep it simple.

9. Keep it to one page.

EXERCISE: *Memo Editing*

Following is a memo sent by the President of XYZ Company to all employees. Revise this memo to make it clearer, shorter, and friendlier. Turn to page 93 for a suggested revision.

MEMORANDUM

TO: All Employees

FROM: The President

DATE: September 15, 19XX

RE: Staff Meeting

XYZ Company wishes to inform all employees of the postponement of the previously scheduled staff meeting. This cancellation is due to the fact of a current pressing financial situation of this company.

This firm has faced a significant drop in the sales volume for the past six months. Our response to these pressing issues must be to make more productive use of our time and effect an increase in the sales volume.

This staff meeting will be postponed immediately until further notice by the president. Employees will be informed of further developments regarding rescheduling our meeting and our financial situation.

EXERCISE (continued)

MEMORANDUM

      TO: All Employees

  FROM: The President

  DATE: September 15, 19XX

      RE: Staff Meeting

HOW TO BEGIN A BUSINESS LETTER

Sometimes, no matter how long you stare at the blinking cursor on your otherwise blank computer screen, you can't figure out how to begin the letter you're trying to write. When this happens to you, a good starting point is to write these words:

I want to tell you that . . .

Next, tell what you want to tell; finally, delete the six words above and see what you have left. These steps can at least get you started, so you'll have something to revise and polish. Here's an example.

---

1. Dear Dr. Ames:

I WANT TO TELL YOU THAT . . .

2. Dear Dr. Ames:

I WANT TO TELL YOU THAT we need to reschedule your tax appointment for an earlier time on Friday.

3. Dear Dr. Ames:

~~I WANT TO TELL YOU THAT~~ We need to reschedule your tax appointment for an earlier time on Friday.

Now this writer can continue the letter to provide additional information, such as the reason for the change (if necessary), a suggested alternative appointment time, etc.

EXERCISE: *Letter Editing*

Although you probably will be spending a lot of time writing, you may find yourself spending even more time editing. As you move up through the managerial ranks, you're likely to edit letters, memos, and reports that were written by others.

The following exercise offers some practice in editing letters. Read through the three paragraphs below; then edit directly on the letter to make it clearer, more concise, and grammatical. You may rewrite sentences, but make sure that the original meaning is not lost. After you finish your revision, turn to page 95 for a suggested revision of this letter.

AJAX BOATS

March 16, 19XX

Annette Clark
Marketing Director
Central Coast Boat Fabrics
1493 Main Street
Morro Bay, CA 93442

Dear Annette:

Thank you for bringing to are attention your product. Kevlar is a good material to make boat hulls out of because it is not heavy like other hull fabrics and since it is used to make bulletproof vests and tank armor it is strong. It is difficult to punctuate a boat made of kevlar.

Unfortunately, kevlar is expensive and kevlar is very difficult to work with due to it's strength. We at the present time do not have the necessary tools to work with this fabric.

For now, we will continue to construct the boats that we make out of fiberglass. As soon as we are ready for kevlar, however, you can be sure that your company will be carefully considered as a kevlar supplier.

Sincerely,

A.J. Smith

PART

IV

Beyond the Basics: Writing for Special Circumstances

SPECIAL KINDS OF BUSINESS WRITING

Congratulations on your progress! Now that you've practiced the basics, we're going to progress to the next level. In this section, you'll have the opportunity to learn how to write for two kinds of events: when you have to convey bad news and when you want to be persuasive.

WRITING BAD NEWS

Whether you're rejecting an applicant for a job, turning down an employee's request for a raise, or breaking the news to a customer that you're out of widgets, writing bad news is not fun—but it's often necessary. And doing it well can help you keep good business relationships.

In the first part of this section, you'll learn some of the strategies and techniques to conveying bad news tactfully, clearly, and kindly.

WRITING PERSUASIVELY

Another kind of business writing that requires special handling is persuasive writing. A lot of business writing is persuasive: cover letters that accompany resumes are designed to sell the applicant, sales letters are designed to sell the product, proposals are designed to sell services, reports are often designed to sell recommendations or solutions to problems.

The last part of this section will show you how to develop your writing to make it more persuasive.

CONVEYING BAD NEWS TACTFULLY

Often in business we must break bad news to good people. This is one time where brevity takes a back seat to tact. Your tone is important. Choose your words carefully; select words that are courteous and positive. Don't use qualifiers, passive construction, or euphemisms to avoid accepting responsibility. For example, a company president wrote the following to her employees:

> *It is necessary to resize our operation to the level of profitable market opportunities.*

What she meant was this:

> *We must lay off staff.*

Note the difference between the following positive and negative phrases:

NEGATIVE	POSITIVE
You failed to notice	*May I point out that*
You neglected to mention	*We also can consider*
You overlooked the fact	*One additional fact is*
You missed the point	*From another perspective*
If you persist in	*If you choose to*
I see no alternative but	*Our clear plan of action*

A memo to correct an employee's behavior is more effective if sentences begin with a word other than "you." Whenever possible, avoid overusing "you."

How to Say No

At times we must deny an employee's request. Be direct and considerate, but don't be too subtle; otherwise, you may mislead by offering false hope instead of communicating clearly. Remember: even criticism can be delivered positively.

SAMPLE BAD NEWS MEMOS

One of your employees has been eagerly awaiting a transfer to the company's San Francisco office. You have been asked to write a memo to tell him the transfer will not take place.

BEFORE

> TO: John Williams
> FROM: Marsha Brown
> DATE: May 12, 19XX
> RE: Denial of your request for transfer
>
> I regret to inform you that your request for transfer to our San Francisco office has been denied. At this point in time, there are no positions open for which you are qualified. Thank you for your understanding.

IMPROVED

> TO: John Williams
> FROM: Marsha Brown
> DATE: May 12, 19XX
> RE: Response to transfer request
>
> After we spoke last week, I checked into the possibility of your transferring to our San Francisco office. Unfortunately, I learned a transfer is not possible for two reasons. First, our department needs your experience and skills for new product marketing. Second, this year San Francisco is expanding its accounting department only.
>
> I am sorry your proposed transfer did not work out. Please let me know if I can assist you in any other way.

Note the difference in packaging. Both memos deny the request, but the "before" version sounds mechanical, stuffy, and cold. Although you want to be clear and concise in your writing, don't sacrifice kindness. When you must give bad news, take the time to select words that are tactful and kind.

EXERCISE: Writing a Bad News Memo

For this exercise, let's say you manage an employee who seems to lack motivation. The employee arrives late to work, dresses inappropriately, and does not finish assigned tasks. In the space below or on a separate sheet of paper, write a memo to the employee to motivate him or her. Supply additional information (such as names) as needed. See page 96 for a suggested solution.

EXERCISE: Writing a Bad News Business Letter

You should now be prepared to write a complete letter using the information you've learned. Refer to the preceding sections as you organize your thoughts, and remember to avoid the common pitfalls of business writing. After you write your letter, turn to page 97 and compare it with the author's example. Although your letter will be different from the model, it will be well written if you avoided unnecessary words, jargon, or vague words. Use the space below to begin your outline.

INSTRUCTIONS: *Write a letter to Mark Smith, who has applied for a position with your firm. Keep the following points in mind: your letter will be rejecting him, he has good qualifications, and you would like more information about him should another position open.*

(You should outline and/or draft your letter on a separate sheet.)

58

NOTE: This page may be used to copy the final version of your letter.

WHEN THE NEWS IS
ESPECIALLY SENSITIVE

A few years ago, a manager in a large company was given the following assignment. A key assistant in the public relations department of the company had been on sick leave for several weeks. This assistant had just been diagnosed with AIDS and had asked the manager to write a memo to all staff—with full disclosure of the illness—to prepare them for the assistant's return to work on the following Monday. Here's the memo.

MEMORANDUM

TO: All Staff
FROM: Paul Henry, PR Manager
DATE: February 15, 19XX
RE: David McDermott's Return

As most of you know, David McDermott has been a key member of our Public Relations staff for nearly three years, and in his new role as Assistant Manager, he continues to provide the timely, quality support that we've all come to depend on since his arrival in our group. Now it's our turn to show him just how supportive we can be.

David has asked me to inform you that he was recently diagnosed with AIDS. After consulting with his doctor, he received approval to return to work, and he'll resume his position on Monday, February 26. David and his doctor assure us that he is completely capable of fulfilling his duties as Assistant Manager. In addition, after consulting with several AIDS experts, we are confident that his return to work will in no way jeopardize the health of any other employees.

I know that you share my feelings of concern for David, and I hope that you will help him in any way possible when he returns. If you have questions or concerns, please contact me or Anna Chin in Human Resources.

Note how clear, kind, and concerned the manager sounds for both his assistant as well as for the other employees.

WRITING PERSUASIVELY

Some people avoid using the word "persuasion" because it conjures images of manipulation and deceit. This is unfortunate because most communication is persuasive. Anytime you influence or affect people you're being persuasive, and everything you write in business—memos, invoices, or client proposal letters—affects the reader.

This section provides information on communicating persuasively and offers you an opportunity to write a persuasive letter using the skills you have acquired in this book.

Here is good first rule: show how your reader will benefit. Don't tell your clients how great your photocopier is—tell them how great their copies will look.

Aristotle said, "The fool tells me his reasons, but the wise man persuades me with my own."

MOTIVATED SEQUENCE: ONE APPROACH TO WRITING PERSUASIVELY

The Motivated Sequence Outline (described on page 62) is effective when you prepare a persuasive letter, report, or speech. Read through each step, then turn the page and review the sample essay that follows the Motivated Sequence Outline.

You should test the effectiveness of your persuasive letters by applying the five steps of the Motivated Sequence Outline. If your letter gets the attention of the readers, shows the readers how a problem affects them, solves the problem, explains what your solution will do, and encourages readers to adopt your solution, then you have written an effective, persuasive letter.

MOTIVATED SEQUENCE OUTLINE

I. Attention Step

A. Overcome readers' apathy

B. Use illustration, example, etc.

II. Need Step

A. Show why change is needed

B. Show why readers *need* to feel affected by the problem

III. Satisfaction (of Need) Step

A. State solution

B. Demonstrate that solution is logical, sensible, and feasible

C. Convince that solution will solve problem

D. Give examples where solution has worked

IV. Visualization (of Future) Step

A. Show readers what solution will do for them

B. State advantages

V. Action Step

A. Convince readers to adopt solution

B. Tell readers what you want them to do

C. Direct readers to act

> *Purpose:* On a separate sheet of paper, write a complete sentence stating exactly what you hope to accomplish in your letter. This gives *you* focus. As you write your letter, remember your purpose to keep your message on track.

Sample Sales Letter

ELITE TRAVEL AGENCY
333 CALIFORNIA STREET
SAN FRANCISCO, CA 94111

April 19, 19XX

Ms. Kathleen Atwood
204 London Street
Oakland, CA 94605

Dear. Ms. Atwood:

(ATTENTION)
If you don't like romance, beautiful places, and friendly people, stop reading now.

(NEED)
But if you need to get away from the pressures of work and school . . . if you would enjoy the exhilaration of bicycling through green pastures and rustic villages . . . if you want to be welcomed with open arms by people known for their warm hospitality . . . then a guided bicycle tour through Ireland, one of Europe's most breathtaking countries, is for you.

(SATISFACTION)
Elite Travel is offering discount prices for students—like you—who wish to spend a splendid summer vacation experiencing a new culture in a foreign land—at prices so low you can't afford to pass it up. Prices for 10-day tours begin at only $4,979, including airfare, bike rentals, three meals per day, and lodging.

(VISUALIZATION)
Imagine bicycling on well-maintained trails, stopping at points of historical interest and incredible views, including castles, battlegrounds, and lands where old Irish tales come to life. Each day we'll stop, tired and happy, at favorite bed and breakfast inns for delicious meals, hot baths, and luxuriating sleep.

(ACTION)
If this package sounds good, call us today. Join us for a vacation you will talk about for years. Call toll free at 1–800–555–0900 before this offer ends on April 30. Don't miss out! We are going to have a great summer, and we'd love to have you along.

Sincerely,

Dan Edwards
Manager

EXERCISE: "Attention Step"—The Sales Letter

A well-written "attention" paragraph is crucial to encourage your reader to read through to the last paragraph (often called the "action" paragraph). Many people, however, find it difficult to write the opening paragraph to any letter—particularly if the letter is persuasive. Once you successfully develop your opening ideas, your remaining thoughts usually flow more naturally.

To give you practice in writing an attention-getting opening paragraph, here is an exercise. Let's say that you are opening a gourmet cafe that serves breakfast and lunch on a university campus. In the space below, write an opening paragraph that introduces your cafe. Remember, your goal in the first paragraph—the attention paragraph—is to arouse the interest of both students and university faculty. Since you have two audiences (students and faculty), try to select strategies that will appeal to both.

_____

_____

_____

_____

_____

_____

_____

_____

_____

_____

After you finish writing your paragraph, read on to see alternative ways of developing a first paragraph designed to grab the attention of your audience.

Sample #1

Dear Students and Faculty:

Are you tired of eating the same old greasy hamburgers and fries? Or tasteless vending machine food? Does eating on campus remind you of eating on an airplane? Does "campus food" sound like an oxymoron? Prepare for a change!

Announcing the opening of *Campus Cuisine*, the first on-campus gourmet cafe that offers tantalizing tastes for finite finances.

Sample #2

Dear Students and Faculty:

Imagine walking to class and experiencing the aroma of freshly baked breads and hearty, flavorful soups. Picture yourself sitting at a cozy table enjoying a rare roast beef sandwich, or spinach and lentil soup with a fresh sourdough baguette, or grilled swordfish with fennel, capers, and sun-dried tomatoes.

Campus Cafe is now open—right here on campus—to serve you delicious dishes at just-right prices.

Note how each of these examples includes specifics to appeal to students and faculty. Typically, students are on budgets, so mentioning reasonable prices would be a sound strategy to appeal to students who have little money. And if it's true that a wider variety of food, including more exotic fare, would appeal to an older, more sophisticated crowd (like a university faculty), describing tantalizing-sounding foods might pique their interest.

Note, too, the *style* of each opening paragraph. Paragraph #1 uses a sentence fragment—incomplete sentence—to make a point ("Or tasteless vending machine food?"). In most professional writing, complete sentences are more appropriate than sentence fragments. But in a sales letter designed to capture attention, formal rules of writing tend to bend a bit.

The second letter includes descriptions that appeal to the senses ("freshly baked," "rare roast beef"). Arousing your readers' senses so they can almost see, hear, taste, or smell can be a good attention-getting strategy.

P A R T

V

Know Your Audience

COMMUNICATION STYLES

Before you begin to write, you need to consider your audience. If you have some insight into the personality of your reader, you'll have the opportunity to tailor your writing to make it compatible with that personality. What could be more flattering to a reader than to receive a letter or memo written with him or her in mind? The addition of a "human element" is so often missing in the business world.

To begin, you must analyze your readers' characteristics. Following are descriptions of four communication styles, which are based on Carl Jung's theory.

SENSOR/ACTION STYLE

People who are strong in this style like action: doing, achieving, getting things done, improving and solving problems.

- *Description:* action-oriented, results-oriented, task-oriented, workaholic, confident, hard-charging, determined, tough, competitive.

- *Strengths:* pragmatic, assertive, directional, competitive, confident, disciplined in using time, receptive to options.

- *Weaknesses:* domineering, arrogant, status-seeking, emotionally cold, impulsive, autocratic, inattentive, impersonal.

- *Common jobs:* athlete, manager, executive, coach, truck driver, entrepreneur, pilot, doctor.

- *Opposite style:* IDEA

COMMUNICATION STYLES (continued)

THINKER/PROCESS STYLE

People who are process-oriented like fact finding, organizing, and setting up strategies and tactics.

- *Description:* analytical, logical, self-controlled, stubborn, detail-oriented, aloof, critical, skeptical, conservative, noncommittal.

- *Strengths:* perfectionist, well organized, objective, rational, conceptual, persistent, accurate, orderly, hard working.

- *Weaknesses:* indecisive, insensitive, inflexible, slow, judgmental.

- *Common jobs:* accountant, banker, attorney, doctor, scientist, clerk, engineer, computer programmer, teacher.

- *Opposite style:* PEOPLE

OBSERVATIONS: These two styles are common in the business world. They have different approaches to understanding and appreciating letters. Above all, the process style wants thoroughness and detail; the action style wants to know the bottom line. Consider the communication style of your reader in everything you write.

FEELER/PEOPLE STYLE

Individuals who are people-oriented like to focus on social processes, interactions, communication, teamwork, social systems, and motivation.

- *Description:* emotional, caring, introspective, melancholic, sympathetic, diplomatic, persuasive, entertaining, warm, friendly, agreeable, dependable, stable.

- *Strengths:* spontaneous, persuasive, empathic, probing, loyal, warm, supportive, dependable, sensitive.

- *Weaknesses:* impulsive, sentimental, procrastinating, subjective, oversensitive, overly cautious.

- *Common jobs:* nurse, secretary, teacher, social worker, sales associate, psychiatrist, trainer.

- *Opposite style:* PROCESS

INTUITORS/IDEA STYLE

People with the idea orientation like concepts, theories, exchanges of ideas, innovation, creativity, and novelty.

- *Description:* creative, reflective, quiet, scholarly, reserved, conceptual, intelligent, enthusiastic, personable, gregarious, impatient, involved, assertive.

- *Strengths:* original, conceptual, warm, approachable, stimulating, adventurous, sensitive, receptive to new ideas, creative, idealistic, flexible.

- *Weaknesses:* unrealistic, devious, impractical, manipulative, undisciplined in use of time, uncontrolled.

- *Common jobs:* scientist, researcher, artist, professor, writer, corporate planner, advertising person, stock broker.

- *Opposite style:* ACTION

OBSERVATIONS: People and Idea styles are becoming more common in the business world. Your letters to readers possessing these traits need to be human. Because so much business writing seems mechanical and computer-generated, the People and Idea styles will appreciate it if you remember that writing is a personal transaction between people.

Let's see how this might work if we take the sales letter from page 63 and adapt it to each communication style.

ACTION STYLE

ELITE TRAVEL AGENCY
333 CALIFORNIA STREET
SAN FRANCISCO, CA 94111

April 19, 19XX

Ms. Kathleen Atwood
204 London Street
Oakland, CA 94605

Dear Ms. Atwood:

Get away from the pressures of work. Recharge your batteries. Do it today. Right now.

Bike through Ireland.
Stop at castles and battlegrounds.
Work up an appetite for excellent meals.
Revel in hot baths and down comforters.
Gear up for the next day's trek.

Elite travel is offering busy people who like action and luxury—people like you—a travel package that costs so little you won't be able to pass it up.

You can join us for a 10-day tour, including airfare, bike rental, three meals per day, and lodging—for only $4,979.

If this package sounds good, call us today. 1-800-555-0900. This offer expires on April 30. Don't miss out.

You've worked hard. You've earned it.

Sincerely,

Dan Edwards

To adapt your writing for the action style, you'll want to emphasize action, doing, achieving, getting things done, improving, and solving problems. Get to the point quickly. Don't waste their time. Be clear and specific.

PROCESS STYLE

ELITE TRAVEL AGENCY
333 CALIFORNIA STREET
SAN FRANCISCO, CA 94111

April 19, 19XX

Ms. Kathleen Atwood
204 London Street
Oakland, CA 94605

Dear Ms. Atwood:

If saving money *and* getting away to a place that will recharge your batteries doesn't appeal to you, stop reading now.

On the other hand, if you need to get away from the pressures of work and school and you would enjoy the exhilaration and education of bicycling through the historical wonders of the Irish countryside, then a guided bicycle tour through Ireland may be just for you.

If bicycling sounds too rigorous for a relaxing, restorative vacation, you have the option of signing up for the accompanying bus trip—your choice.

Elite Travel is offering discount prices for people like you—people who would like to vacation in Ireland and experience a new culture at prices so low you can't afford to pass it up. Prices for 10-day tours are $4,979, including airfare, bike rental or bus fare, three meals per day, and lodging.

You can find all the details about this package in the enclosed brochure. But remember: This offer expires on May 15.

If this sounds good, call us tool free at 1-800-555-0900. We'll be glad to answer all your questions. Don't miss out. Join us for the vacation of a lifetime!

Sincerely,

Dan Edwards

To adapt your writing for the process style, emphasize facts, organizing, and structure. Provide more detail than for other styles. Appeal to logic and reason.

PEOPLE STYLE

ELITE TRAVEL AGENCY
333 CALIFORNIA STREET
SAN FRANCISCO, CA 94111

April 19, 19XX

Ms. Kathleen Atwood
204 London Street
Oakland, CA 94605

Dear Ms. Atwood:

If you don't like romance, beautiful places, and friendly people, stop reading now.

On the other hand, if you need to get away from the pressures of work and school and you would enjoy the exhilaration of bicycling with other enthusiastic students through green pastures and rustic villages, if you want to be welcomed with open arms by people known for their warm hospitality, then a guided bicycle tour through Ireland, one of Europe's friendliest and most breathtaking countries, is for you.

Elite Travel is offering discount prices for people like you—people who would like to experience a new culture at unbeatably low prices. Prices for 10-day tours are $4,979, including airfare, bike rental, three meals per day, and lodging.

Throughout this tour we will bicycle on well-maintained trails, stopping at historical points of interest with incredible views that include castles, battlegrounds, and villages where old Irish tales come to life. Each day we'll stop, tired and happy, at favorite bed and breakfast inns for delicious meals in a family atmosphere, hot baths, and luxuriating sleep.

If this sounds good, call us toll free today at 1-800-555-0900 before this offer expires on April 30. Join us for a vacation that you'll talk about for years. Don't miss out! We're going to have a terrific vacation, and we'd love to have you along.

Sincerely,

Dan Edwards

To adapt your writing to the people style, emphasize social processes, interactions, communication, and teamwork.

IDEA STYLE

ELITE TRAVEL AGENCY
333 CALIFORNIA STREET
SAN FRANCISCO, CA 94111

April 19, 19XX

Ms. Kathleen Atwood
204 London Street
Oakland, CA 94605

Dear Ms. Atwood:

If you don't like romance, beautiful places, and friendly people, stop reading now.

On the other hand, if you would enjoy the exhilaration of bicycling through green pastures and rustic villages, if you want to be welcomed with open arms by people known for their warm hospitality, then a guided tour through Ireland, one of Europe's friendliest and most breathtaking countries, is for you.

Imagine . . .
    bicycling on well maintained trails,
        stopping at historical battlegrounds,
            enjoying incredible views of castles, and
                visiting villages where old Irish tales come to life.

Each day we'll stop, tired and happy, at favorite bed and breakfast inns for delicious meals, hot baths, and luxuriating sleep.

Elite Travel is offering discount prices for people like you—people who would like to experience an adventure of a lifetime. Prices for 10-day tours are $4,979, including airfare, bike rental, three meals per day, and lodging.

If this sounds good, call us toll free today at 1-800-555-0900 before this offer expires on April 30. Join us for a vacation that you'll talk about for years. Don't miss out! We're going to have a terrific vacation, and we'd love to have you along.

Sincerely,

Dan Edwards

To adapt your writing to the idea style, emphasize theories, exchange of ideas, innovation, creativity, and novelty.

REVIEW

For a general review, the facing page offers a summary of the most important points discussed in this book. You might find it helpful to refer to this page often, particularly the "Ten Techniques for Effective Communication." Make it a habit to read through the list to incorporate these techniques whenever you practice writing.

At first, you may find that old habits die hard, and that when you attempt to improve your writing, it will take you longer to write even routine letters. You may be tempted still to use jargon and clichés. You may become frustrated as you stare at a blank pad or as your wastebasket fills with crumpled paper. Don't despair! Writing is hard work, but the quality of the final product is the key to greater rewards.

Good luck!

A useful companion book is *Writing Business Proposals and Reports* by Susan Brock, Crisp Publications: Menlo Park, CA. 1992.

Ten Techniques for Effective Communication

1. Keep your writing clear, concise, and simple.

2. Choose your words carefully.

3. Be natural.

4. Avoid fad words, jargon, and clichés.

5. Use active verbs, avoid passive construction.

6. Take a stand, make a commitment, avoid qualifers.

7. Use familiar words—plain English.

8. Be specific: avoid vagueness.

9. Eliminate redundant expressions.

10. Keep your audience in mind.

ENTER A LEARNING CONTRACT

A definition of "accountability" is to be responsible for one's actions.

We all have good intentions. The thing that separates those who are successful from those who are not is how well these good intentions are carried out.

A voluntary contract (or agreement) can help convert your good intentions into action.

The Voluntary Learning Contract on the facing page is a good starting point if you are serious about getting the most from this book.

This agreement can be initiated by you or your supervisor before you begin working in this book or after you have completed it.

CONSIDER A VOLUNTARY CONTRACT

VOLUNTARY
LEARNING CONTRACT

I, _____ , agree

(Your Name)

to meet with the individual designated below at the times shown to discuss my writing skills progress. The purpose of all sessions will be to review my writing skills and establish action steps in areas where improvement may still be required.

I agree to meet with the above individual on:

_____

_____

_____

_____

(described schedule giving date and times)

_____

Signature of supervisor or instructor

Areas needing attention:

☐ Spelling

☐ Punctuation

☐ Usage

☐ Style

☐ Writing Persuasively

☐ Other

_____

My Signature   *Date*

P A R T

VI

Solutions to
Exercises

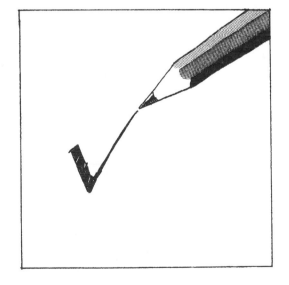

SOLUTION TO SPELLING EXERCISE (PAGE 8)

1. Many companies want to hire people who are <u>FLEXIBLE</u> (flex-ble).

2. Ms. Brown wanted us to sit <u>TOGETHER</u> (tog-th-r) at the meeting so we would not be <u>SEPARATED</u> (sep-r-ted) when the meeting was over.

3. The new hotel can <u>ACCOMMODATE</u> (acco-date) up to 1,500 guests.

4. This memo <u>SUPERSEDES</u> (super-edes) the <u>PRECEDING</u> (prec-ding) one, which was distributed last week.

5. The hospital <u>BENEFIT</u> (ben-fit) raised a lot of money for the children's wing.

6. It never <u>OCCURRED</u> (oc-ur-ed) to us that the <u>GOVERNMENT</u> (gove-ment) might increase our taxes.

7. The secretary's boss <u>OFFERED</u> (of-er-ed) her a bonus if she would <u>PROCEED</u> (proc-d) to enroll in a shorthand class.

8. We avoided an <u>ARGUMENT</u> (arg-ment) when we discussed changing the <u>ENVIRONMENT</u> (envi-ment) of the office to boost employee morale.

9. The hinges on the door are <u>LOOSE</u> (l-se), and it <u>CONSISTENTLY</u> (consist-ntly) rattles when opened.

10. It would be difficult not to <u>BELIEVE</u> (bel-ve) the results.

SOLUTION TO PUNCTUATION EXERCISE (PAGE 14)

1. The executive watched the competition, but the competition went ahead with the takeover.

2. During our meeting she was genial but shrewd.

> No punctuation needed. The introductory phrase is short and doesn't require a comma. Note there is no comma before the phrase "but shrewd" because it is not an independent clause.

3. Today more women are becoming executives in corporations.

> No punctuation needed.

4. The job was difficult; therefore, he quit.

> *OR:* The job was difficult. Therefore, he quit.

> *OR:* The job was difficult, and therefore he quit.

5. My suitcase contained files, pencils, books, and paper.

> NOTE: There is no colon after "contained" because a colon must follow a complete sentence such as the following:

> "My suitcase contained four items: files, pencils, books, and paper."

6. We thought we would have to work late; consequently, we were happy to be home before dark.

> *OR:* We thought we would have to work late. Consequently, we were happy to be home before dark.

7. My boss's car was in the shop; however, she borrowed her husband's.

8. In preparation for the meeting, Mr. Jones asked us to do three things: set up the equipment, dust the tables, and empty the ashtrays.

9. We wanted to go to the partners' meeting, but we were unable to leave before the weekend.

10. Lois's résumé arrived yesterday; moreover, she phoned for an interview next week.

SOLUTION TO SPELLING AND PUNCTUATION EXERCISE (PAGE 15)

Punctuation corrections are circled; spelling errors are lined out and corrected.

Southwestern Corporation 333 LaSalle Street, Chicago Illinois

March 29, 19XX

Mr. John C. Fremont
2929 East Sycamore Street
Chicago, IL 60601

Dear Mr. ~~Freemont~~: Fremont:

Thank you for meeting with us, and for your time and effort in preparing for the ~~intervue~~ interview. We appreciate your ~~accomodating~~ accommodating us with a ~~flexable~~ flexible schedule.

We are in the final stages of ~~procesing~~ processing your application, and we need three more items for our files: your social security number, permanent home address, and your date of birth. As soon as we get this information, we can ~~proceede~~ proceed to complete your permanent records.

Everyone here at Southwestern Corporation is looking forward to working with you, and we are eager to have you begin as soon as possible. Please, call me as soon as you can with this information.

Sincerely,

Janet L. Estes
~~Senor~~ Senior Vice President

/jle

SOLUTION TO A USAGE QUIZ (PAGE 16)

1. Which is correct?

> The **effect [result]** of wearing seatbelts can **affect [influence]** the number of people injured in automobile accidents.

Effect can be used as noun or a verb. As a noun, it means "result" or "outcome." As a verb, it means "to bring about."

"Affect" is usually used as a verb in business writing, and it means "to influence."

2. Which is correct?

> Lee Iacocca singlehandedly **effected** [brought about] the turnaround of Chrysler Corporation, which had a dramatic **effect** [outcome] on the production of U.S. made automobiles.

3. Which is correct?

> **a.** The party pledges not to raise taxes, which would be harmful to the economy.
>
> **b.** The party pledges not to raise taxes that would be harmful to the economy.

The correct answer depends on the meaning. The first choice (a) is correct if the party pledges not to raise any taxes (because raising any taxes would be harmful to the economy). The comma sets off nonessential elements in the sentence (see Punctuation Pointers), which means that the clause that follows the comma is not essential to the meaning of the sentence.

Second choice (b) says that the party will not raise any taxes harmful to the economy (implying that the party could raise taxes not harmful to the economy). To as a taxpayer, the difference between (a) and (b) could be important.

4. Which is correct?

A historic choice.

5. Which is correct? Depends on the meaning.

> **a.** He implied that we were not to blame. (Implied means suggested. Speakers imply.)
>
> **b.** He inferred that we were not to blame. (Inferred means concluded. Listeners infer.)

6. Which is correct?

This memo will **supersede** the one we wrote last week.

7. Which is correct?

There **seem** to be problems with the way management has handled billings.

Problems is plural; therefore, "seem" is correct.

8. Which is correct?

Neither my boss nor the partners **go** to the meetings.

Although generally a singular verb follows "neither" and "either," if one of the subjects is plural and one is singular, make the verb agree with the subject nearer to it. "Partners" is plural and is nearer to the verb.

9. Which is correct?

The **effect** of lower interest rates will **affect** our money market investments.

10. Complete each sentence using either *capital* or *capitol*.

Austin is the **capital** of Texas.

The company tried to raise enough **capital** to buy new equipment.

Paris is the **capital** of France.

The first word of every sentence should begin with a **capital** letter.

The senator met with the press on the steps of the **capitol** building.

Use "capitol" only when you refer to the building itself.

SOLUTION TO WORDINESS EXERCISE 1 (PAGE 28)

terminate the illumination	lights out
revenue commitment	tax increase
at this point in time	now
in the event of	when
due to the fact that	due to or because
at a later date	later
jumped off of	jumped off
on a daily basis	daily
each and every one	all
firstly	first
in my opinion, I think	use one or the other (or none, since opinion is implied
irregardless	regardless
owing to the fact that	due to or because
there is no doubt but that	undoubtedly or doubtless
so very happy	happy
clenched tightly	clenched
close proximity	close
close scrutiny	scrutinize
in the majority of instances	usually
at this juncture of maturation	now
in an intelligent manner	intelligently

SOLUTION TO WORDINESS EXERCISE 2 (PAGE 28)

1. I have always wanted to go into accounting because it challenges me.

2. I believe Smith ignored the consultant's suggestion.

3. Many of our West Coast competitors have gone out of business because of the recession.

4. It is company policy to carefully test all new products for effectiveness.

5. If Wilkins does not help us financially, we may not be able to acquire needed raw materials.

SUGGESTED SOLUTIONS TO PASSIVE VOICE (PAGE 31)

Revise the following sentences so that all main verbs are in the active voice. Leave the space blank if the sentence is already in the active voice.

1. Our request for an increase in salary will be considered by the board at its next meeting.

> *At their next meeting, the board will consider our increase in salary.*

2. Our inability to agree is seen by management as a weakness.

> *Management sees our inability to agree as a weakness.*

3. The decision on the annual budget is always made by our board of directors.

> *Our board of directors makes the decision on the annual budget.*

4. Incorrect data on the computer should be deleted.

> *We should delete incorrect data on the computer.*

5. Our office manager will speak to us on Monday.

> [OK as is. Needs no revision.]

6. It will be necessary to downsize the company's marketing department.

> *We need to lay off part of the company's marketing department.*

7. Problems should be reported to the office manager.

> *Report problems to the office manager.*

8. The check was signed by my boss.

> *My boss signed the check.*

9. Please be advised that these adjustments should be completed immediately.

> *Please complete these adjustments immediately.*

10. The jobs were completed by the management team.

> *The management team completed the jobs.*

SOLUTION TO PARALLEL WRITING EXERCISE (PAGES 33–34)

1. It was both a <u>long</u> and <u>very tedious</u> meeting.

2. Joe likes a job with <u>challenging and stimulating</u> work. OR
Joe likes a job <u>that challenges</u> him and <u>that keeps</u> him stimulated.

3. Poor writing <u>wastes</u> time, <u>costs</u> money, and <u>alienates</u> customers.

4. <u>Speaking in</u> public is sometimes harder than <u>writing in</u> private.
[No change needed]

5. My partner is a man of <u>action</u>, <u>decision</u>, and <u>intelligence</u>.

6. This would eliminate <u>continual errors</u>, <u>repeated corrections</u>, <u>unnecessary memos</u>, <u>and</u>, most important, <u>wasted time</u>.

7. His experience made him <u>sullen</u>, <u>bitter</u>, and <u>cynical</u>.

8. Our instructor <u>drilled</u> us, <u>tested</u> us, and <u>encouraged</u> us.

SOLUTION TO PARALLEL WRITING EXERCISE (continue)

9. I went to Maui <u>to enjoy</u> the warm weather and <u>to practice</u> snorkeling.

10. I <u>plunged</u> into the water, <u>swam</u> away from shore, and <u>made</u> my <u>first dive</u>.

11. Our first choice is John, who is <u>healthy</u>, <u>witty</u>, <u>capable</u>, and <u>athletic</u>.

12. The personnel officer told me that the clerk would <u>answer</u> the phone, <u>greet</u> visitors, <u>distribute</u> mail, and <u>type</u>.

13. On a resume:

Hobbies: swim<u>ming</u>, read<u>ing</u>, cycl<u>ing</u>, and play<u>ing</u> the piano

14. On an overhead transparency during a business presentation:

WHAT WE CAN DO FOR YOU:
<u>Increase</u> your cashflow
<u>Improve</u> your customer relationships
<u>Reduce</u> employee turnover
<u>Develop</u> new business

15. Sometimes, <u>going</u> to meetings is as exciting as <u>watching</u> paint dry.

[No change needed]

SUGGESTED REVISION TO MEMO EDITING EXERCISE (PAGE 47)

MEMORANDUM

TO: All Employees

FROM: The President

DATE: October 15, 19XX

RE: Staff Meeting Postponement

To help get our sales volume back on track, we are postponing our staff meeting until early winter. We will let you know our meeting's new date as soon as we select it.

I appreciate your extra efforts and encourage you to be productive and work to increase sales during the 4th quarter.

This revision is just one approach to improving the memo. Here, the president uses a more personal tone ("We" instead of "XYZ Company" and "You" instead of "employees"). Using active (instead of passive) voice helps keep the information simpler, clearer, and shorter.

SUGGESTED REVISION TO LETTER EDITING EXERCISE (PAGE 50)

DRAFT

AJAX BOATS

March 16, 19XX

Annette Clark
Marketing Director
Central Coast Boat Fabrics
1493 Main Street
Morro Bay, CA 93442

Dear Annette:

Thank you for bringing to ~~are~~ *our* attention (your product) Kevlar is a good material ~~to make~~ *for* boat hulls ~~out of~~ because it is ~~not heavy like~~ *lightweight* ~~other hull fabrics and since it is used to make bulletproof vests and tank armor it is~~ strong *and* ~~It is~~ difficult to ~~punctuate a boat made of kevlar~~ *puncture*.

(Unfortunately, Kevlar is expensive and ~~kevlar is very~~ difficult to work with due to it~~'~~*s* strength. *Currently* ~~We at the present time~~ do not have the necessary tools to work with this fabric.

For now, we will continue to construct ~~the~~ *our* boats ~~that we make~~ out of fiberglass. As soon as we are ready for kevlar, however, ~~you can be sure that~~ *we will consider* your company ~~will be carefully considered~~ as a Kevlar supplier.

Sincerely,

A.J. Smith

FINAL

AJAX BOATS

March 16, 19XX

Annette Clark
Marketing Director
Central Coast Boat Fabrics
1493 Main Street
Morro Bay, CA 93442

Dear Annette:

Thank you for bringing your product to our attention. Kevlar is a good material for boat hulls because it is strong, lightweight, and difficult to puncture. Unfortunately, Kevlar is also expensive and difficult to work with due to its strength. We do not have the necessary tools to work with this fabric.

For now, we will continue to construct our boats out of fiberglass, but as soon as we are ready for Kevlar, we will consider your company as a Kevlar supplier.

Sincerely,

A.J. Smith

SUGGESTED SOLUTION TO WRITING A BAD NEWS MEMO EXERCISE (PAGE 56)

MEMORANDUM

TO: John Smith

FROM: Maria Jimenez

DATE: September 11, 19XX

RE: Performance Update

As I look back over your work during the past six months, I'm convinced you can succeed in our marketing department. Recently, however, some of your work habits haven't been up to your usual high standards. Specifically, I'm referring to punctuality, appropriate dress, and timely task completion.

PUNCTUALITY: Arriving to work on time (8:00 AM) is extremely important to client service—especially when our clients are accustomed to calling us early knowing their account manager will be here.

APPROPRIATE DRESS: Professional dress (as described in our Employee Handbook) from Monday through Thursday (with casual dress on Friday) is important, especially for those unexpected business presentations and client meetings.

TIMELY TASK COMPLETION: Deadlines are a constant here, so our general rule is if you know you will not be able to complete a task on time, inform your supervisor immediately so that we'll have the time to assign the task.

John, please see me if you have questions; otherwise, I'm confident you'll get back on track this week. Let's meet on October 15 to follow up on and these and other topics.

Notice how Maria describes the positive behaviors she wants to see (instead of a more negative "inappropriate dress," "tardiness," and "not completing tasks").

SUGGESTED SOLUTION TO WRITING A BAD NEWS BUSINESS LETTER EXERCISE (PAGE 57)

August 14, 19XX

Mr. Mark Smith
100 Elm Street
Glenville, WA 98888

Dear Mark:

Thank you for applying to XYZ Corporation for the position of staff accountant. Although we do not have any openings now, we expect to interview again in December. Your resume is impressive, and we will keep it on file if a staff accountant position should become available before December.

Meanwhile, please send us three letters of recommendation to complete your application package. We appreciate your interest.

Sincerely,

XYZ CORPORATION

by William R. Houghton

NOTES

NOTES

NOTES

NOTES

Now Available From

Books•Videos•CD-ROMs•Computer-Based Training Products

If you enjoyed this book, we have great news for you.
There are over 200 books available in the *50-Minute™* Series.
To request a free full-line catalog, contact your local distributor or
Crisp Learning
1200 Hamilton Court
Menlo Park, CA 94025
800-442-7477
CrispLearning.com

Subject Areas Include:

Management

Human Resources

Communication Skills

Personal Development

Marketing/Sales

Organizational Development

Customer Service/Quality

Computer Skills

Small Business and Entrepreneurship

Adult Literacy and Learning

Life Planning and Retirement

CRISP WORLDWIDE DISTRIBUTION

English language books are distributed worldwide. Major international distributors include:

ASIA/PACIFIC

Australia/New Zealand: In Learning, PO Box 1051, Springwood QLD, Brisbane, Australia 4127   Tel: 61-7-3-841-2286, Facsimile: 61-7-3-841-2618
ATTN: Messrs. Gordon

Philippines: National Book Store Inc., Quad Alpha Centrum Bldg, 125 Pioneer Street, Mandaluyong, Metro Manila, Philippines   Tel: 632-631-8051, Facsimile: 632-631-5016

Singapore, Malaysia, Brunei, Indonesia: Times Book Shops. Direct sales HQ: STP Distributors, Pasir Panjang Distrientre, Block 1 #03-01A, Pasir Panjang Rd, Singapore 118480   Tel: 65-2767626, Facsimile: 65-2767119

Japan: Phoenix Associates Co., Ltd., Mizuho Bldng, 3-F, 2-12-2, Kami Osaki, Shinagawa-Ku, Tokyo 141   Tel: 81-33-443-7231, Facsimile: 81-33-443-7640
ATTN: Mr. Peter Owans

CANADA

Crisp Learning Canada, 60 Briarwood Avenue, Mississauga, ON L5G 3N6 Canada
Tel: (905) 274-5678, Facsimile: (905) 278-2801
ATTN: Mr. Steve Connolly/Mr. Jerry McNabb

Trade Book Stores: Raincoast Books, 8680 Cambie Street,
Vancouver, BC V6P 6M9 Canada
Tel: (604) 323-7100, Facsimile: (604) 323-2600   ATTN: Order Desk

EUROPEAN UNION

England: Flex Training, Ltd., 9-15 Hitchin Street,
Baldock, Hertfordshire, SG7 6A, England
Tel: 44-1-46-289-6000, Facsimile: 44-1-46-289-2417   ATTN: Mr. David Willetts

INDIA

Multi-Media HRD, Pvt., Ltd., National House,
Tulloch Road, Appolo Bunder, Bombay, India 400-039
Tel: 91-22-204-2281, Facsimile: 91-22-283-6478   ATTN: Messrs. Aggarwal

SOUTH AMERICA

Mexico: Grupo Editorial Iberoamerica, Nebraska 199, Col. Napoles, 03810 Mexico, D.F.
Tel: 525-523-0994, Facsimile: 525-543-1173   ATTN: Señor Nicholas Grepe

SOUTH AFRICA

Alternative Books, PO Box 1345, Ferndale 2160, South Africa
Tel: 27-11-792-7730, Facsimile: 27-11-792-7787   ATTN: Mr. Vernon de Haas